Facilitation Skills

90 Minute Guides

Michelle N. Halsey

ISBN-10: 1-64004-021-8
ISBN-13: 978-1-64004-021-2

Contents

Chapter 1 – Understanding Facilitation

Facilitation is often referred to as the new cornerstone of management philosophy. With its focus on fairness and creating an easy decision making, facilitation can make any organization make better decisions. This workshop will give participants an understanding of what facilitation is all about, as well as some tools that they can use to facilitate small meetings.

At the end of this tutorial, you should be able to:

- Define facilitation and identify its purpose and benefits.

- Clarify the role and focus of a facilitator.

- Differentiate between process and content in the context of a group discussion.

- Provide tips in choosing and preparing for facilitation.

- Identify a facilitator's role when managing groups in each of Tuckman and Jensen's stages of group development: forming, storming, norming, and performing.

- Identify ways a facilitator can help a group reach a consensus: from encouraging participation to choosing a solution.

- Provide guidelines in dealing with disruptions, dysfunctions, and difficult people in groups.

- Define what interventions are, when they are appropriate, and how to implement them.

Recall the last time you had a group meeting. The group meeting can be at work, at church, at civic groups or even within the family.

Think about the way the meeting was ran, the person (or people) who steered the discussion, and the tools and techniques used to engage the participants and accomplish all the meeting's goals.

The following guided questions can help this process:

In your group:

1. Did you feel that everyone's contribution is welcome?

- What are your indicators?

- What did the facilitator (this maybe you) say or do to make the group feel welcome or unwelcome?

2. Did you feel that the decisions your group made are reflective of everyone's position, or at least the best compromise of everyone's position?

- What are your indicators?

- What did the facilitator (this maybe you) say or do to make surface everyone's point of view and incorporate it in the decision-making process?

3. Which of these two do you think is prioritized more in your group: getting the tasks in the agenda accomplished, or making the most of the knowledge, creativity, and relationships in the group? What makes you say so?

Understanding Facilitation

Groups are powerful resources in any organization. When you tap into groups, you don't just get the best of individual members, you also get the best of group interaction. The result is a more dynamic, creative and empowered team.

To get the most of groups, you need facilitation skills. In this module, we will discuss what is facilitation, what is a facilitator and when is facilitation appropriate.

What is Facilitation?

Facilitation is a manner of handling group meetings in a way that takes the focus away from just one leader, and instead distributes leadership to all members of the group. There is premium on democracy, group involvement, and cooperation. The focus is not just on getting things done, but also in feeling good about it.

Consultant Dave Sibbet defines facilitation as *"the art of leading people through processes towards agreed-upon objectives in a manner that encourages participation, ownership, and creativity from all involved."*

Facilitation is often contrasted with presentation, which is delivering information or decisions to a group. Facilitation is group-centered while presentation is leader-centered. For this reason, facilitation is incompatible with an autocratic management style.

Example of the difference between facilitation and presentation:

FACILITATION: *"How do you think the company can solve this problem? Does anyone have any ideas?"*

PRESENTATION: *"This is how we will solve the problem..."*

What is a Facilitator?

Group-centered meetings require an individual or individuals in the case of larger groups to manage the process. This person(s) is a facilitator.

A facilitator is a person who helps groups to arrive at their objective by ensuring that everyone's contribution is heard and the processes being used are both productive and empowering to all. Facilitators work primarily through leading and blocking techniques, basically directing traffic within a group discussion. Facilitation can also involve managing group member's emotions, defusing tensions and encouraging team cohesiveness. In some cases, facilitators help in setting and revising meeting structure, and managing conflicts.

To be effective, facilitators have to be neutral to the discussion, not partial to any members, and acceptable to everyone involved. They should not take a position in any of the issues raised, nor should they advocate a solution --- or attempt to directly solve the problem. Having an objective "third party" facilitator ensures that group members would feel safe about voicing out their opinions.

Knowledge of group process and an appreciation of democratic management are pre-requisites to becoming an effective facilitator. Sensitivity and keen observation skills are also non-negotiable.

When is Facilitation Appropriate?

In general, facilitation has something positive to offer every group process, whether we're talking about a working group or a recreational group.

Facilitation is most appropriate:

When you want to encourage group motivation, commitment and confidence. A facilitated process is a great way to get employees engaged and empowered; it sends the message that all team members' opinions, suggestions, and feelings are valued, and will at least be taken into consideration before making a decision. When a discussion is facilitated, group members can take pride in the results, because the bulk of the ideas came from them.

More so, a facilitated process promotes ownership of a task or an issue among group members. Because results depend directly on the team members' effort and performance, teams are more likely to invest in the process and carry a task through.

When you want to make the most of group knowledge, experience and diversity. Facilitation is ideal when you have people of different backgrounds, expertise and or work style, and you want to create something that integrates all these differences. For example, brainstorming sessions always work best if participants are from diverse disciplines. Facilitation can ensure that all members have their say, and that cross-fertilization of ideas (members building on other members' ideas) can happen.

When there is more than one answer to a question, or one side to a story. Facilitation is appropriate for discussion of issues that allow a healthy debate and multiple perspectives. A discussion where the solution is clear from the very beginning, or where no other viable alternative exists, is not recommended for facilitations. Similarly, a conflict situation where only one position will be tolerated is not for facilitation.

When a person in power wants to just be a participant.
Facilitation is recommended when a leader wants to level off with his members when discussing an issue. For example, a discussion on a sensitive policy change is best handled by a neutral facilitator; so that

members don't feel intimidated or threatened by their boss' position, and boss' can be guided in seeing things from their employees' point of view. Facilitation is also advisable when a person in power wants a fresh perspective, and he's worried that he'll influence output if he leads the discussion.

When you want to learn about your group's process, or challenge an inefficient process. Facilitation can be a way to identify roots of unproductive discussions, and teach alternative ways of tackling an issue. For example, meetings that often monopolized by one person can be restructured by simply adding a facilitator. Once that group experiences a facilitated discussion, they might be inclined to have more democratic meetings even after the facilitator leaves.

When there are psychological blocks that need to be addressed in an issue. A discussion might seem clear cut, with decisions final. However if there are underlying tensions and reservations, calling in a facilitator will be a good idea. Facilitators are experts in not just managing what was said, but what was left unsaid as well. He or she can surface psychological blocks to an issue and bring it to discussion.

Facilitation is least appropriate:

When discussing issues where the only solution is administrative adjudication. Some issues are not meant for discussion but for an executive decision, an example of this is the termination of an employee. Also, if two parties are at a stalemate and the only way to resolve the issue is for the leader to directly interfere and make a judgment call, then mediation is more appropriate than facilitation.

When the goal of a meeting is merely to inform a group. Facilitation is not recommended in situations when group members don't have the information or sometimes authority, to get the task done. The same goes when group members are in no position to contribute to the issue for ethical or legal reasons. In these cases, information can only flow from the leader down to the members and not vice-versa.

When participants take turns in arriving at the meeting. Group-centered discussions require continuity, which is why it should only be appropriate to situations where all or a significant number of group members are available for meeting at the same time. If a group is always changing members in the middle of a discussion, or only one "clique" or coalition in a group is present, it is difficult to conduct effective processes.

In crisis situations when quick decisions have to be made. Facilitated discussions take significantly more time than non-facilitated discussions, and arriving at a consensus is not always guaranteed. If quick decision-making and immediate action is required, facilitation is not recommended.

Chapter 2 – Process versus Content

Facilitators are process experts; they are as interested in the "how?" as much as the "what?" To produce quality output, you must arrive at it functionally. In this module, we will discuss the difference between process and content, and which among the two should be a facilitator's focus.

About Process

Process refers to the way a discussion is happening, independent of the subject matter or issue being talked about. Basically, process talks about how a group works together. It includes how members talk to each other, how they identify and solve problems, how they make decisions, and how they handle conflict. It takes into account group dynamics, non-verbal messages, and situational elements.

Process elements include:

- **Meeting Flow.** How does the meeting begin? How do they transition to another item in the agenda? Who keeps the ball rolling? Are there topic jumps? How does the meeting end?

- **Participation.** How many people contribute to the discussion? What is the quality of their contribution? Are there highs, lows, and shifts in group participation? How are silent people treated?

- **Communication.** How do group members communicate with one another? Is the verbal communication congruent with the non-verbal communication? Who talks with whom? Who interrupts whom?

- **Roles.** What roles do each member of the group play? Are these roles self-assigned or assigned by others? Are the roles productive? How do the members of the group respond to these roles?

- **Power/ Influence.** Who has high influence? Who can move the group into a particular action whether positive or negative? How do they exert this power? Is the group democratic, authoritarian, or permissive when it comes to discussions? Are there shifts in power/influence? Are there rivalries? Do there seem to be coalitions and alliances?

- **Problem-Solving Process.** Is the problem stated in clear workable terms? Does it seem clear to everyone what the issue is? How does the group arrive at solution? Is this method acceptable and fair to all members?

- **Decision-Making Process.** How are the best interests of all participants represented in the decision making process? Are there self-authorized decision-makers? Does the group arrive at a consensus? Is the way of deciding acceptable to all members of the group? How are people who disagree with the majority treated?

- **Group Atmosphere**. What is the general feeling in the group? How are feelings handled? Are they encouraged and validated? Is this group capable of care? Are there significant emotional attachments between members?

About Content

Content refers to the subject matter of a discussion: the actual words or ideas that were spoken independent of contextual variables like non-verbal cues and procedural variables. It refers mainly to the literal meaning of words and makes no reference to connotations, subtexts, and insinuations behind messages.

In a meeting, content is the agenda topic, the suggestions put forward by the staff members, the solutions they arrive at. Content in a facilitated discussion should *all* come from the group and not the facilitator.

Example: The content of the meeting may be "how to change the company's image to that it will appeal to a younger market." In contrast the process element in the same meeting is brainstorming to solicit as many options as possible.

A Facilitator's Focus

Which between process and content should a group facilitator attend to?

Ideally, a facilitator should attend to both process and content. After all, process and content feed one another. Good meeting processes create better content; keeping to relevant content makes for a great discussion process. A productive discussion can only happen when the content is on track and the meeting flows in a functional way.

However, facilitators are primarily process experts; they manage information flow and treatment. They are not encouraged to provide content input in any way. While some knowledge of a meeting's topic can help a facilitator manage a meeting better, a facilitator should not put forward personal opinions and suggestions, or make judgments and decisions for the group. They're also content neutral; they should never take sides in a debate.

When a facilitator adds to the content of a discussion, the facilitator's role is confused from neutral guide to biased participant or a trainer/coach. If a content expert is needed (one whose task is to clarify technical issues in a discussion e.g. a lawyer for union issues, or an Organizational Development consultant), they can be included as participant in the group for expert reference.

Here is an example of a facilitator focusing primarily on process instead of content:

Imagine that a group discussion is stuck. The group can't seem to generate a good, viable idea for their project. A content expert in this situation can provide a range of alternatives they can try--- after all he or she has specialized knowledge in this area. But a facilitator is a process expert. Instead of giving suggestions, a facilitator would seek to identify why idea generation is not proceeding well. Maybe the group is tired? Maybe the problem needs to be re-defined? In these cases, a facilitator can encourage a working break to get the thinking juices flowing, or ask the group to re-define the problem to encourage a different perspective, respectively.

Chapter 3 – Laying the Groundwork

A facilitated approach is not just a technique; it's an attitude and disposition to doing things that should be shared by the whole organization. To best benefit from group facilitation, you need to set the stage for it. In this module, we will discuss choosing a facilitated approach, planning for a facilitated meeting and collecting data.

Choosing a Facilitated Approach

In an earlier module, we discussed about the situations where facilitation is appropriate and situations when facilitation is not appropriate. These factors can be a guide if facilitation is the best approach to managing a meeting in your organization.

If your organization has decided that facilitation is appropriate, the following are some steps you should take:

Orient the participants about what facilitation is, and what it can do for them. If a team is new to the facilitated approach, they might find difficulty with the process. For example, individuals from a hierarchal organization might feel uneasy contributing when there are senior members in the group. In situations where there's conflict, the group might even expect the facilitator to adjudicate the issue or at least offer an opinion. It's important then to level everyone off with what facilitation is (and what it isn't) before you start implementing it in your group. If there are significant reservations about changing to a facilitated approach, surface them so that they may be addressed.

Make sure that facilitation has the administration's support. The incentive to make the most out of a facilitated discussion can be nullified if the people who make decisions still prefer a top-down, autocratic approach. While it's not guaranteed that ideas and proposal produced by facilitated teams will get approved, administration should at the very least communicate their openness to the team's efforts.

Choose the right facilitator. Facilitators can be from within the organization or a freelance professional.

It is important that you pick a facilitator who is not part of the problem-context or the solution, and is generally perceived as unbiased with no conflict of interest. They must also possess the right attitude and disposition in handling people's contribution.

Planning for a Facilitated Meeting

The following are some things you can do in preparation for a facilitated meeting:

Set the venue. Facilitation works best if the venue is conducive to a comfortable discussion. Chairs arranged in a circle are always better than a classroom set-up, to emphasize equality among all members. Privacy is a must. If you need to use materials like flip chart paper, markers, and nametags, prepare them beforehand.

It also helps to prepare not just the venue of the meeting proper, but the surrounding areas as well. It's not unusual for facilitators to invite meeting participants to break out in smaller discussion groups, or even "take a walk" to blow off steam. As such, preparations for these activities should be made before the meeting.

Set aside time. Facilitated meetings should not be rushed; minding process is the reason why it works well. The length of a facilitated meeting depends on the agenda and the number of participants, but the recommended duration is 30 minutes to one hour.

Prepare a Facilitation Plan. As a facilitator, never go blindly into a meeting. While an experienced facilitator would likely have enough skills enough to "wing it", it always pays to be prepared.

Make sure you know what the objective of the meeting is, expectations of the group and/or the organization from you, and the profile of your participants. Decide ahead how you are going to begin and end the meeting, and how you plan to manage the meeting itself. For this process, it helps if you research and gather relevant information beforehand (more on this later), and prepare a Facilitation Plan (see the next page).

Make plans for documentation. To better be able to follow up, and identify process issues in a group, it always helps if a meeting is documented. Typically, groups assign a secretary to take minutes of a meeting. However, traditional minutes usually deal with just content.

For best results, consider assigning a process observer: someone to document process elements in a group.

Prepare Psychologically. Lastly, it's important that you take the time to prepare internally if you're going to facilitate a meeting. Being a facilitator can be a mentally, sometimes even emotionally, demanding job. You want to make sure that you are in a relaxed frame of mind before you facilitate. Deal with personal issues that can interfere with the process, and note your biases and assumptions about the group or the subject of the meeting.

Below is a sample template for a Facilitation Plan:

Participants:	
Beginning Time:	**Ending Time:**
Meeting Topic(s):	

Meeting Objectives:
  A.
  B.
  C.	

Icebreaker or Opener:	
Discussion Questions:	**Discussion Method:**
Summary/ Integration:	
Evaluation:	

Collecting Data

The more information a facilitator has about the group she will be facilitating, the more effective he or she can be.

The following are some tips in collecting data as preparation for facilitating a meeting:

- Communicate ahead with the person who invited you to facilitate the meeting to understand what is expected from the meeting and what is expected from you as a facilitator. If there are presenters and content experts in the meeting, it's also best to meet with them beforehand to ensure that you are both on the same page.

- Ideally, you should also be able to interview or survey participants ahead of time. This can give you time to understand the dynamics of the situation, as well as establish rapport. Ask about the group's history, their view of the meeting subject, and how the group normally accomplishes things. It also helps to know ahead if there are reservations about inviting a facilitator.

- Request documentation about the group's previous meetings e.g. minutes or progress reports. They will give you an idea of where the group is at the moment.

- If there's a sensitive issue involved, know as much as you can about the situation – and even the personalities involved. For instance, knowing that there's underlying tension about a specific topic will tell you to approach it cautiously. Similarly, knowing who the participants in conflict are can guide you when dividing participants into working groups. Note though: always triangulate your information gathering method so that you don't get just one side of the story.

- Understand the subject matter of the meeting. While facilitators are not content experts, you must know enough about the topic to be able to track the discussion. For example, familiarize yourself with the terms and language of the group. You lose precious time by having to ask the group to explain terms to you.

Chapter 4 – Tuckman and Jensen's Model of TeamDevelopment

Groups are not stagnant entities; they change. Initial uncertainty and ambiguity give way to stable patterns of interaction, while relationship between members wax and wane. To be an effective facilitator, you must be sensitive to the changes happening within groups.

In this module, we will discuss one of the most widely-used theories of group development: Tuckman and Jensen's Model of Team Development. We will also discuss how a facilitator can best respond to groups depending on what stage of development they are in.

Stage One: Forming

The initial stage of group development is the forming stage. It is commonly referred to as the orientation stage or the *"getting-to-know-you"* stage, as group members still don't know much about each other or about the organization. If the organization itself is new, then there might not be any existing structure or rules in the group yet.

During the forming stage, members tend to feel tensions and uncertainties. After all, group members are dealing with people they hardly know, and this initial unfamiliarity may leave them feeling uncomfortable and constrained. Often, members are on guard, carefully monitoring their behavior to make certain they avoid any embarrassing lapses of social poise.

Without the benefit of a long and solid relationship with the group, involvement and commitment to the organization may be low. There may also be extreme dependence on leaders, dominant personalities and other group members.

The forming stage is characterized by many tentative and testing behaviors: explorations of the boundaries of both rules and tasks.

During the forming stage, it is important for the facilitator to:

• Establish rapport among group members

- Encourage members to be comfortable with one another

- Make everyone feel accepted in the group

- Establish rules and guidelines for both task and relational behavior

- Encourage the group to be comfortable with the organization

Stage Two: Storming

A natural offshoot of uncertainty and ambiguity is the need to clarify expectations, establish patterns, and put a structure into place. Clarity, patterns, and structure are what make a group stable. However with many different personalities and perspectives to reconcile, these things don't always evolve smoothly. The natural formation of sub-relationships within the group can also add to the pressure. Enter the second stage of group development: the storming stage.

The storming stage of group development is characterized by conflict, whether overt fighting or subtle tensions. This happens when at least two people disagree on a way of doing things or a way of relating. Conflicts in groups also occur when particular members assert control or dominance in some form, and other members resist. Coalition-building and fractionalization of the group can happen as members take sides on an issue.

The emotional atmosphere in groups during the storming stage can be characterized by tension, anger, frustration, and discounting of other people's responses.

A facilitator guiding a team in the storming stage should remember that conflict is normal, even necessary element, in group development. Conflicts are signs that there are processes that need streamlining, or issues that require a definite response. When conflicts surface within groups, facilitators can help the group see an opportunity to set a structure (which is the next stage.)

During the storming stage, it is important for the facilitator to:

- Defuse tensions

- Promote positive communication in the group

- Identify problems areas

- Facilitate conflict resolution processes

Stage Three: Norming

The third stage of group development is the norming stage.

If the conflict areas during the storming stage are addressed properly, the result should be the establishment of norms.

Norms are rules or standards of behavior within a group. They can be explicit (such as a company policy) or implicit (unspoken expectations). Norms help groups to meet their goals. At the very least, norms help the group maintain some degree of stability so that tasks can be done.

During the norming stage, group members develop greater cohesiveness and possibly intimacy. There is greater security in opening up to others and suggesting new ways of doing things. The norming stage is a period of clarity in terms of the group's identity, dynamics, and direction.

If you're a facilitator handling a group in the norming stage, it helps to:

- Practice skills in identifying possible solutions

- Define roles and expectations

- Manage change

- Help the group to reach a consensus

Evaluating new systems and protocols, and making revisions if necessary are also part of the norming stage.

Stage Four: Performing

When groups are able to successfully implement a new rule or system, they can begin a period of optimum productivity. With stability in place, there is room for creativity, initiative, stability, open relationships, pride, learning and high morale. Group energy is no longer taken up by set-up matters, and can be channeled fully to the work. The group goes into the height of task success: the performing stage.

The relationships among group members also become more relaxed and involved. Because the task details are already clearly defined, and there is no need for vicious power struggles, there is more room for closeness and deeper relationships among members.

To get to the performing stage is the goal of all organizations. As a facilitator, your task is to guide the group towards this stage. One important thing to remember though is that optimal productivity often occurs later in a group's life, and a period of storming and norming are pre-requisites to it.

At this stage, the role of the facilitator is to help maintain the group in the performing stage. Tasks include providing support and motivation in each task, and reinforcing best practices.

What happens if the group gets new members or encounters new tasks? What if a new issue comes about threatening peak performance? In these cases, the group can go back to earlier stages. For example, if new groups members make pre-existing rules obsolete, or a new conflict area is spotted, then the group returns to the storming stage to hash out a new system. It is said that in the life course of a group, it will return to the storming stage regularly. See figure in the next page.

An effective facilitator can point out that that re-accomplishing developmental tasks characteristic of earlier stages (e.g. establishing rapport) may be needed to adapt to new changes.

An Illustration of Tuckman and Jensen's Stages of Team
Development:

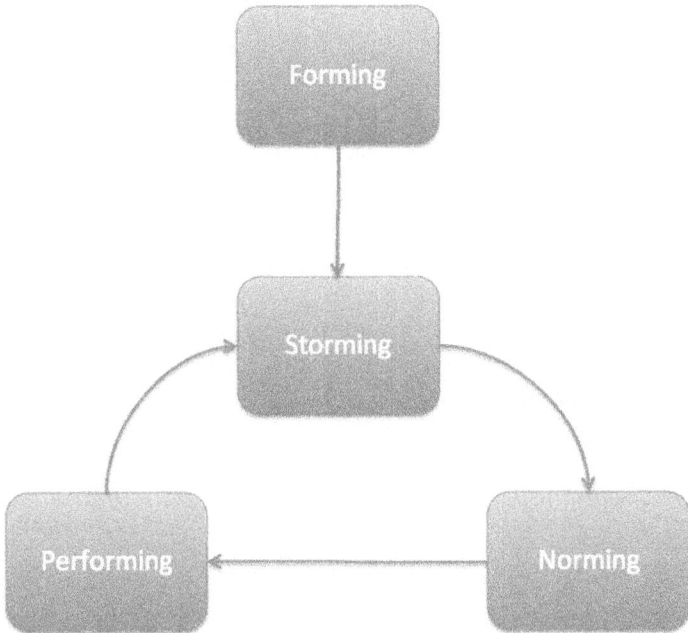

Chapter 5 – Building Consensus

The aim of facilitated discussions is to create participatory groups: one where the goal is cooperative rather than competitive decision-making. All members should have equal input in the process, and equal opportunity to voice opposition to an idea or conclusion. In this module, we will discuss the key facilitation skills needed to build consensus: encouraging participation, gathering information, presenting information, synthesizing and summarizing.

Encouraging Participation

Consensus is more likely to happen if members feel encouraged to contribute. The following are some of the ways a facilitator can encourage participation in small groups:

Provide preparation guidelines in the meeting agenda. Participants are more likely to contribute, if they feel confident that they have something to add to the discussion. It's helpful then to send out a meeting invitation with guidelines what to review and study in preparation for the meeting. It is also better if you can also send out guide questions ahead of time.

Before starting a group meeting, check on everyone's comfort level. Some people are at ease being in meetings; others have difficulty. There are also situational factors, such as an uncomfortable seat or a poorly ventilated room, which can hamper group participation. Inquiring if group members are comfortable before starting a meeting can help a facilitator establish rapport with the group, and address hindrances to group participation.

State at the start of the meeting that members' participation is not just welcome, but is integral to the process. Sometimes, all it takes is for the facilitator to explicitly say that members are allowed and encouraged to participate for the discussion to be a lively one. These guidelines can be made part of the orientation process.

Acknowledge responses. Show that you have heard and understood a contribution. You can do this in non-verbal and verbal ways. Non-verbal ways include eye contact, nodding, and leaning forward towards the speaker. Verbal ways include praising ("I'm glad you brought that up.", "That's a good point."), clarifying (If I may reiterate what you just said, you suggested that, is this correct?), and requesting for more information ("Tell us more.", "Please go on.").

Avoid discounting responses. Similar, make sure that you're careful not to give a response that might be interpreted as devaluing a contribution, or even ignoring it. Examples of discounting responses are "That was said already." , "That's irrelevant." , "That's it? Is there anything else?"

Solicit group members' responses. You can encourage participation by directly asking everyone their opinion on a subject matter. Example: "Can I get everyone's opinion about this proposal?" or "Let's share all our ideas. We won't react until we've heard them all."

Build on responses. A good way to encourage participation is to integrate each member's response with that of other members or with the whole group. Similarities and differences are surfaced, and the way each point relates to another is verbalized. This way, the discussion is moving and the individual contributions are seen as relevant to the whole.

Ways to do this include:

- **Universalizing** – Helping the group see that their concerns are shared. Example: "Who else has felt this way?"

- **Linking** – Making verbal connections to what individual members say and feel. Example: "Bill thinks that there should be another meeting to prepare for the conference. This seems to be similar to what April was saying a while ago." Or "Michael believes that the group should outsource all customer communication. Jonathan, on the other hand, feels that an in-house customer care staff will serve the company better. It seems we have two different but equally valid approaches to this problem."

- **Redirecting** – To promote the involvement of all in the discussion. Example: "What do you think about that?" or "What do you think about Mark's idea?"

Intentionally keep silent. Intentional silence can also be a way to encourage participation, especially if a group is eager to contribute and needs no prompting.

Thanking the Group. Lastly, affirming the group for their participation, and each member for their contribution, can encourage greater involvement in the succeeding meetings.

Gathering Information

The following are some of the ways a facilitator can gather information during a discussion.

Go-round. In this technique, each member of the group gets a turn to speak without getting interrupted. Sometimes, the amount of time each member is allowed to speak is limited to encourage fairness. In go-rounds, each member gets to speak. Note that this method may not be applicable if you have many participants.

Break Out Groups. In this technique, the facilitator divides the participants into smaller groups (anywhere from dyads up, depending on the size of the group and the subject to be discussed) and then later allots time for a representative from each group to share their point of view. This method is applicable when there are too many participants to do an efficient go round, or some discussion is necessary, but that discussion is more effective in smaller teams.

BRAINSTORMING. Brainstorming is a method of gathering information that involves getting as many ideas from the group in limited time. During brainstorming, participants can verbalize any idea they have, good or bad, and a documenter logs it in a flip chart. Only when all the ideas have been exhausted, or there are already enough ideas for consideration, does the group check out each idea one by one. For best results the time for brainstorming is limited.

FISHBOWL Method. This method is best when an intense discussion of a subject is needed, but the group is too large for the time allotted. In the fishbowl method, a sample of the group discusses the topic, while the rest function as observers. Ideally, the discussion sample should represent the diversity in the group.

Presenting Information

In order for a discussion group to reach a consensus, it is important that they are well-informed of the facts of the issue, as well as the positions of the different parties concerned. In this sense, an effective facilitator is one that can guide group members in presenting important information to the plenary.

The following are some tips in presenting information in groups.

Separate presentation from discussion time. Assign a time particularly for presentation of information. Going back and forth between discussion and presentation can disrupt group process and may even make for ineffective decision-making. For best results, place the presentation time on the agenda, and assign presenters before the meeting proper.

If there are more than one side to an issue, or more than one option in consideration, make sure you assign equal time for each. Process can be helped if each party feels that they are being treated fairly. Being given equal time as another party can facilitate this. And even if there are no conflicting parties in the group, giving each subject or each proposal the same time as the others can ensure that decisions that would be made at the end of the meeting are not biased in any way.

Use a multi-media guide if possible. When presenting information, it helps to know that information can be presented in visual (the use of colorful presentations, hand-outs, demonstrations, flipcharts, videos, etc.), auditory (descriptive narratives and reports) and bodily/kinesthetic (activities to learn key points) ways. Use the method that fits the learning style of the group and the subject of the presentation.

Note that the use of projected visual aids may require a darkened room, making the meeting less conducive for group interaction.

Synthesizing and Summarizing

A synthesis is an integration of key points or key process movements in the discussion. An example of synthesizing is listing issues that have been resolved and issues that are still up for discussion. A summary, on the other hand is a short recap of what has been discussed or what has happened. Syntheses and summaries are not just conducted at the end of each meeting, but also during the discussion proper.

Synthesizing and summarizing key discussion points is facilitative during a meeting. There are many reasons for this. First, synthesis and summaries show that the discussion is on track and following the agenda. It can also clear confusing discussions, and help members see where the group is at any moment. These processes also give the group a sense of accomplishment --- the synthesis and the summary is usually an indication of movement in the discussion.

The following are some ways a facilitator can synthesize or summarize during a group discussion:

- Let the group summarize or synthesize for themselves. Example: Ask group members "What have we discussed so far?", "What did you learn from this discussion?" or "What have we decided about this situation?"

- Ask a group member/ group members to provide a synthesis or summary.

- Offer your tentative synthesis/ summary and seek for the group's clarification. For example: "This is what we have discussed so far....Did I miss anything?"

- Refer to the agenda or published documentation in a flip chart paper. "So far, we have discussed Topic A and B. These are our resolutions..."

Chapter 6 - Reaching a Decision Point

The steps outlined in the previous module are just ways to set the stage towards consensus-building. When it comes to the actual decision point, it helps that a facilitator knows ways to guide a group towards optimal decision-making. In this module, we will discuss ways to identify options, create a short list, and choose a solution. We will also use a way of deciding not often considered by many, called the multi-option technique.

Identifying the Options

The following are some ways groups can identify options during decision-making. Some of these ways are also the ways of gathering information discussed earlier.

Brainstorm. Brainstorming is the process of coming up with as many ideas as you can in the shortest time possible. It makes use of diversity of personalities in a group, so that one can come up with the widest range of fresh ideas. Quantity of ideas is more important than quality of ideas in the initial stage of brainstorming; you can filter out the bad ones later on with an in-depth review of their pros and cons.

Round Robin. Ask each member of the group to suggest one option for consideration. All members must contribute an idea.

Facilitated SWOT Analysis. Some teams create each option as a group, and they do so by conducting a facilitated analysis of the organization's strengths, weaknesses, opportunities and threats, as they relate to the problem.

The most import thing about these processes is that they are conducted in a consultative fashion.

Creating a Short List

There are many criteria a facilitator uses to help a group create a shortlist. The following are just some of these ways:

• **Costs and benefits.** An ideal solution is one that has the least costs and most benefits.

- **Disagreeing parties' interests**. An ideal solution has factored in the impact on all parties concerned and has made adjustments accordingly.

- **Foresight**. An ideal solution doesn't have just short-term gains but long term ones as well.

- **Obstacles.** An ideal solution has anticipated all possible obstacles in its implementation and has made plans accordingly.

- **Values.** An ideal solution is one that is consistent with the mission-vision of the organization and or its individual members.

Choosing a Solution

There are many ways a facilitator can guide a group in creating a shortlist. The following are just some of these ways:

Decide on a criterion (or criteria). Ask the group to come up with the criteria to be used to evaluate each option. These criteria could be costs and benefits, consistency with the values of the organization, feasibility, etc. Once criteria are set, the facilitator can guide the group into weighing each option according to the criteria.

Survey which options members like. A facilitator can also conduct a quick survey of what each group members like in the list. You can select the solution either by strict consensus or by majority vote.

Survey which options members don't like. Similarly, a facilitator can ask the group which options from the short list are no-no's and eliminate them from the list.

Using the Multi-Option Technique

When coming up with solutions to an issue, you are not limited to choosing one best one. You can also pick several solutions to a problem, and follow through on these many solutions simultaneously. This process is called the multi-option technique.

For instance, in addressing a problem about lagging sales, approaches can be related to poor advertising, poor market selection, or a problem in the product itself. A group following the multi-option technique will assign a person or team to follow through on each option. One team can create a better advertising campaign; another team can look for a better market; while another team can improve the product. In succeeding meetings, each team will report their results as separate teams.

The solutions followed through in a multi-option technique are not necessarily complimentary to one another, although groups have the option to follow through on only complimentary ideas. But if the group wants to see two opposing scenarios with different assumptions, they can do so.

How can a facilitator conduct the multi-option technique? The group can brainstorm several options, and the facilitator can help the group select which of the many options they want to pursue further.

Chapter 7 – Dealing with Difficult People

Group process can get hampered by the presence of difficult members. A skilled facilitator should know how to deal with difficult people, so that the discussion will remain on track and the group atmosphere will remain pleasant and conducive to participation. In this module, we will discuss how to address disruptions, common types of difficult people in groups and how to handle them, and how to let the group resolve issues on their own.

Addressing Disruptions

Disruptions in groups can be in any form. They can be from the members, or from the environmental factors.

The following are ways to deal with disruptions in groups:

- **Refocus the discussion on the agenda.** This intervention is similar to the intervention on keeping the discussion on track. If a disruption occurs, gently remind the group of the topic.

- **Identify the intention behind the disruption and address it.** Don't focus on what was said. Instead, focus on why the person said it. Example: repeated interjections can mean that a member does not feel like he or she is being listened to.

- **Reiterate rules.** You may refer to ground rules set at the beginning of the session.

- **If no rule against the disruption exists, then take it as an opportunity to set one.**

Common Types of Difficult People and How to Handle Them

The following are some of the common types of difficult people in groups and how to handle them.

Type of Difficult Person	Description	Typical Behavior	Ways to Deal with Them
Dominating	These are members who monopolize the conversation and even overtly block other members from making a contribution.	*"I am the only one with experience in this matter. Let me tell you what to do."*	• Solicit other members' opinion. *"We appreciate your experience and we'll take what you said into account. But let's see what others think too."*
Aggressive	Members who resort to personal attacks.	*"You just don't know what you're doing!"*	• Reiterate the ground rules. *"We have agreed that there will be no personal attacks."* • Get back on topic. *"Remember all comments are useful as long as they relate to the topic.* • Re-state their position in objective terms
Quiet and Non-Participative	Group members can be quiet for a variety of reasons: they can be shy, intimidated, or uncomfortable joining in the topic.		• Establish eye contact and invite them to join in. *"We'd like to hear from people we haven't heard from before. Could you give us your take on this issue?"*
Overly Talkative	Members talk too much.		• Remind them of the time limit. • Tell them you can only discuss one point at a time. • Ask them for key summary points.

36

Helping the Group Resolve Issues on Their Own

The following are two ways a facilitator can help groups resolve issues on their own:

Ignore. For cooperative teams, natural facilitators will emerge if the facilitator doesn't make immediate interventions.

Promote direct feedback. Ask the group members what they think about the situation or a particular person's behavior. Example: "Mike, can you tell Bob the effect on you when he interrupts you?"

Chapter 8 – Addressing Group Dysfunction

All groups have the potential to be dysfunctional: incapable of achieving goals. This is because each person is different, and each group has their own unique history. A facilitator must know how to recognize signs of group dysfunction, and be skilled to address them. In this module, we will discuss three ways to address group dysfunction: setting ground rules, restatement and reframing issues and keeping the discussion on track.

Using Ground Rules to Prevent Dysfunction

One of the best ways a facilitator can anticipate problems in a group discussion is to set ground rules. Ground rules orient participants with what is expected from them. Moreover, they set boundaries of acceptable and unacceptable behavior during the discussion. For best results, ground rules must be set in a consultative fashion, with the rules, and sometimes the consequences of violation of rules, negotiated among members of the group and agreed upon by consensus.

When setting ground rules, it is important to both verify if the rules are understood, and if they are acceptable. Make sure too that a documentation of the ground rules is available for everyone, either as a hand-out or posted in a flipchart paper for everyone to see.

Ground rules in a group meeting can relate to:

- **How to make the most of the meeting.** For example: practice timely attendance, participate fully.

- **How to make a contribution to the discussion.** For example: do the members raise their hands and ask the facilitator for permission to speak; use I-messages.

- **How members should treat other members**. For example: "don't interrupt whoever is speaking, listen actively to whoever has the floor, accept that everyone has a right to their own opinion, no swearing or any aggressive behavior.

- **Issues relating to confidentiality.** Example: all matters discussed in the group shall remain within the group. This is also the moment for the facilitator to reveal if the minutes of the meeting will remain solely for his or her reference, or will it be given to an authority in the organization.

- **How violations of ground rules would be addressed.** Example: the use of graduated interventions from warning to expulsion from the group.

Restating and Reframing Issues

The way an issue or problem is phrased can influence group members' attitudes towards it. After all, different words have different meanings and connotations. A simple example is the difference between the words "problem" and "challenge" in reference to a situation, or "victim" and "survivor" in reference to a person.

Restatement is similar to paraphrasing; it is changing the wording of an issue, but the main idea is the same. For example: simply changing "this suggestion seems to have made some members of the group angry", to "there seems to be a strong concerns about the suggestion" can lessen the antagonistic nature of the statement.

Reframing is similar to restatement, except reframing goes deeper. In reframing, a facilitator changes the way a problem is conceptualized in order to facilitate a consensus or support a conflict resolution. In some cases, the problem is reframed in order to support the position of two parties in contention. The meaning may or may not change, but the spirit of the statement remains the same. For example, instead of saying "we're here to talk about how to approach salary cuts," a facilitator can say "we're here to talk about how the company can provide employee security despite limited funds."

In group facilitation, simply restating or reframing an issue can lessen the adversarial nature of a position, or invite a fresh way of looking at things. When the issue is phrased in neutral or workable terms, it becomes conducive to a reasonable discussion.

How can a facilitator successfully re-state or reframe an issue? The main skill necessary for these processes is active listening. An effective facilitator must be sensitive to what each party needs and be able to incorporate these interests when phrasing an issue. Having an appreciation of the language of the group, and their unique perspective, are also important in this process.

Some of the ways of restating and reframing includes:

- Changing "hot buttons" or value-laden words into neutral ones.

- Reminding the group of larger goals/ smaller goals the entire group is working on.

- Changing a problem into workable terms.

- Approaching an issue from another perspective.

Getting People Back on Track

A group discussion can go off-topic for many reasons. Sometimes, the purpose of the meeting wasn't really clear. In other times, the discussion naturally led to an interesting issue not part of the agenda. And in other times, there are individuals who initiate and maintain off-topic discussions.

Regardless of the reason, the following are ways to get a discussion back on track:

Review the agenda. A facilitator can create check points in the agenda and constantly refer to it as the discussion progresses. For example: "Let's take a moment to take a process check. Are we still following our agreed upon agenda?"

Reflect to the group what is happening, and reintroduce the correct topic. Example: *"I appreciate the participation and enthusiasm. But it seems that we have gone off the agreed upon agenda. I believe the topic under discussion is..."*

Offer to put the off-topic on a "parking lot" for possible later discussion. For example: "You raised a good point Mary. Maybe we can look at that later it today, or set a separate meeting for it."

Ask the group if they are finding the discussion helpful to the goal. This intervention is recommended for unstructured meetings, where a foray into an off-topic is not necessarily a negative thing. For example: "I noticed that there has been a long debate in the group about this idea. Is this discussion helpful for everyone?"

Ignore the off-topic discussion and reintroduce the correct topic.
If you feel that acknowledging a topic detour will just result in more
dysfunction (e.g. it will provoke a long, defensive response), then it
may be best to just ignore it. Instead, summarize the last thing that
was said related to the topic, and ask a question that continues from it.
For example: "If I may get back to what Louis was saying earlier. He
said....Does anyone agree with his observation?"

Chapter 9 – About Intervention

In general, facilitators neither inject themselves in issues nor direct the flow of discussion; they merely go where the group wants to go. There are occasions, however, when stronger responses are needed to make the group more functional and productive. In this module, we will discuss what these stronger responses are, why they are necessary, and when is it appropriate to use them.

Why Intervention May Be Necessary

Facilitators are part of a group for a reason: to help the group achieve their goals in the most democratic and cooperative way possible. Ideally, groups should have cooperative members with knowledge, skill, and personality to assist this process. However, in the real world, groups are much more complicated. Indeed, even well-meaning group members can create dysfunctional teams. For this reason, intervention may be necessary.

An intervention is an injection of one's self in the process in pursuit of a specific goal. Interventions are what separate a facilitator from a mere participant--- the participant's statements are contributions, whereas a facilitators' statements are interventions.

Technically, anything that a facilitator does, both verbally and non-verbally, in the course of his or her role in a group is an "intervention." However, the term intervention is usually reserved to relatively stronger interference in a group's natural way of doing things.

The following are some of the reasons why intervention may be necessary:

To help the group achieve their goals. If an on-going dynamic in the group is keeping the entire team from reaching their objective, then it's time to intervene. For example: if a coalition exists in members, decision-making might get skewed to one side of the issue.

To protect group process. If the integrity of the chosen methodology in getting results is being compromised, then a facilitator must intervene.

To prevent the escalation of an issue. Generally, facilitators should let the group handle things on their own. But some hot issues are better nipped in the bud, or they might blow up into a larger issue can create serious damage.

To sample "skills" to the group. In some occasions, group members lack the skills to deal with a group issue, e.g. two conflicting issues. In these cases, intervention may be necessary to expose the group on more functional processes.

When to Intervene

The following are some situations when intervention may be necessary:

- The group is stuck. This means that the process is not producing results, or the process is not progressing to the next level.

- The group is about to move on to the next agenda without realizing that an important aspect of the discussion is unresolved or unaddressed.

- The group continues to follow a negative pattern despite soft interventions. (We will discuss levels of interventions in the next section.)

- Something unethical is going on in the group, like a personal attack or subtle/blatant intimidation.

- Group process is being hampered by a dominant person or clique.

- Group members are misunderstanding each other.

- The facilitator perceives tension and suspiciousness in the group.

Levels of Intervention

There is a guiding principle in medicine that goes: don't prescribe strong medicine when a milder one will do. Similarly, interventions in facilitation range from non-directive to directive, subtle to explicit, non-intrusive to very intrusive. It helps to know what the levels of intervention are in order to decide what response to give to different situations in a group.

The following are the different levels of intervention:

No intervention. Unless there is a pressing concern that requires a facilitator's intervention, the first level of response is to do nothing. By not responding to a concern, a facilitator is effectively letting the group take care of the problem, and implement their own solution. Note though that even if a facilitator is not directly responding to the problem, he or she may be actively gathering information about the group and how they process their own issues.

Reflective Technique. The first few levels of intervention are geared towards increasing awareness within the group that a problematic situation is in place. One way to do this is to objectively state what you notice is going on. Note that you are not supposed to voice out your opinions or evaluations of the group dynamic; merely bring to awareness something that the group may not have noticed. The group is left to confirm or refute the facilitator's observations. Either way, the result may be further clarification.

Example: "I noticed that four of you had been very quiet since we started."

Solicit the Group's Observations. As much as possible, let the group members identify themselves what is happening within the group. One way to do this is to solicit feedback through general leads. Example: *"Jane. What can you say about what is happening right now?"*

If general leads are not working, you can use direct leads. Example: "Jane, what can you say about the way the discussion about (subject) is going?

Interpret observations. This becomes necessary when the group has difficulty seeing the implications of what is going on in the process. NOTE: always phrase your interpretations in tentative fashion, as if seeking confirmation from the group if your observations are correct or incorrect.

Example: *"I'm noticing that the energy is low? Are we focusing on the right issue? Or is there something else that we have more energy for?"*

Suggest solutions. If the group seems to be stuck, suggest a way to deal with the problem. Note: suggest only process changes. And always get the approval of the group. Example: "We seem to be stuck, would you like to try a different approach?"

Restructure the process or an aspect of it. Change the group process by re-organizing the structure of dialogue (dyads, small groups, etc.), using problem solving processes, inserting a "process break" or changing the original agenda.

Confront. This is directly mentioning the problem, or the difficult individual. Note that confrontation is a very strong intervention, and must be used only as a last resort, when all other softer interventions have been exhausted.

Example: *"I noticed that you are always encouraging the other members of the group to leave the meeting prematurely. And twice now it has disrupted the process. May I know what the reason why you're doing this is?"*

Chapter 10 – Intervention Techniques

In the previous module, we introduced intervention and the different levels of intervention. In this module, we will focus on particular intervention techniques: use of processes, boomerang it back, and **ICE** it.

Using Your Processes

As process experts, the best way a facilitator can intervene in an unproductive or dysfunctional group is by introducing a process that would directly address the problem or issue.

For example, if a group's problem is the monopoly of the floor by certain members, a facilitator can introduce the round robin discussion to ensure that everyone gets their turn to speak.

If the problem is the lack of information about the issue in contention, the facilitator can make presentation part of the agenda.

If the problem is a lack of understanding between management and staff, the facilitator can break the group into pairs of management and staff.

Boomerang it Back

To "boomerang" an issue back is to present an issue back to the group for them to resolve. The reflective technique (discussed in the previous module) is one of the basic ways of mirroring an issue to a group.

Another way to do this is to rephrase a group's concern into a question addressed to the group. For example, when a group member says "maybe we are just too tired to think of a new idea for this project", a facilitator can simply say *"do you think you are too tired?"*

Or if a group member asks a facilitator a question, the facilitator can just bounce the question back. Example: if a group member asks "should we continue this project?" the facilitator can simply reply *"What do you think? Should you?"*

ICE It: Identify, Check for Agreement, Evaluate How to Resolve

Another way to intervene is to use the ICE technique.

ICE stands for:

- Identify

- Check for Agreement

- Evaluate How to Resolve.

When you ICE it, you surface what the problem is, verify with the group its accuracy (or at least their agreement), and then start the process of looking for solutions.

Example: "What do you think is going on in the group right now? So, if I understand correctly, this is what is happening? Is this correct? How do we go about addressing this problem?"

Additional Titles

The 90 Minute Guide series of books covers a variety of general business skills and are intended to be completed in 90 minutes or less. It is an effective way for building your skill set and can be used to acquire professional development units needed by project managers and other industries to maintain their certification. For the availability of titles please see

https://www.silvercitypublications.com/shop/.

No. 1 - Appreciative Inquiry

No. 2 - Assertiveness and Self Control

No. 3 - Attention Management

No. 4 - Body Language Basics

No. 5 - Business Acumen

No. 6 - Business and Etiquette

No. 7 - Change Management

No. 8 - Coaching and Mentoring

No. 9 - Communications Strategies

No. 10 - Conflict Resolution

No. 11 - Creative Problem Solving

No. 12 - Delivering Constructive Criticism

No. 13 - Developing Creativity

No. 14 - Developing Emotional Intelligence

No. 15 - Developing Interpersonal Skills

No. 16 - Developing Social Intelligence

No. 17 - Employee Motivation

No. 18 - Facilitation Skills

No. 19 - Goal Setting and Getting Things Done

No. 20 - Knowledge Management Fundamentals

No. 21 - Leadership and Influence

No. 22 - Lean Process and Six Sigma Basics

No. 23 - Managing Anger

No. 24 - Meeting Management

No. 25 - Negotiation Skills

No. 26 - Networking Inside a Company

No. 27 - Networking Outside a Company

No. 28 - Office Politics for Managers

No. 29 - Organizational Skills

No. 30 - Performance Management

No. 31 - Presentation Skills

No. 32 - Public Speaking

No. 33 - Servant Leadership

No. 34 - Team Building for Management

No. 35 - Team Work and Team Building

No. 36 - Time Management

No. 37 - Top 10 Soft Skills You Need

No. 38 - Virtual Team Building and Management

www.ingramcontent.com/pod-product-compliance
Lightning Source LLC
Chambersburg PA
CBHW071743020426
42331CB00008B/2153